The First Christmas:
Finding Your Way After Loss

Erica Staab

DEDICATION

To all those who have walked this journey of grief with me…
To all those who have trusted me to walk alongside on your journey…

Thank you from the bottom of my heart.

A Little Book of Healing and Hope

CONTENTS

"Let everything happen to you
Beauty and terror
Just keep going
No feeling is final"

— **Rainer Maria Rilke**

1 THE "MERRY" DILEMMA

Christmas is coming and it brings so much anticipation, so many pieces of joy, of light, and yet for many it brings longing and pain.

You may be one of the many who are in the midst of various in-between's struggling with not feeling the joy, with feeling the pain of feeling disingenuous when saying "Merry Christmas".

The first Christmas after my divorce and the unexpected death of my brother I simply didn't. I stopped saying "Merry Christmas".

The words felt so hollow, the pain so deep, and the gap between the joy of the outside world and the darkness in my heart so wide. I allowed myself to say "you too" and offer a small smile, but there was no "Merry" that year.

I wish someone would have told me that it was okay.

I wish someone would have reminded me that it wouldn't last forever. For right then in those moments there was no "Merry" and that was okay.

I struggled with wanting to feel "Merry". I wanted so desperately to be "normal". I wanted to care, but there wasn't enough energy left no room left in my heart for any "Merry", the grief took up too much room.

My friend who had lost her daughter shared with me about a Christmas card she received. At the bottom of the card a well-meaning friend had written "I hope all is well". Her eyes filled with tears and her voice broke as she shared the unintended pain those words had caused. This is the second year without her daughter to and all is not well. Although she knows that the capacity to feel joy, to see beauty, to share love will increase- right now it is overshadowed by the grief and loss.

Those words stung- a reminder that life is permanently changed, there is a before and after. It is hard to trust that it will ever be "well" again when the loss looms so large.

Other friends are struggling with the desire for "perfect" Christmases when children are melting down, parents nerves are strung tight, and everyone just seems to be overwhelmed and overstimulated. For everyone it can just feel like too much. Often if feels there is the expectation coming from every direction of the need to have the perfect "Hallmark" Christmas.

We all need to remind each other to hold ourselves gently, to know that our efforts are enough, even though it doesn't always feel like it.

The magic of Christmas is that grace weaves its way through the difficult moments,

that often there is a sparkle of light when you least expect it,

and that meaning can be found in the simple moments shared together.

I invite you to remember the most memorable moments of Christmas for you. I doubt they have anything to do with the presents you received or a perfectly cleaned and decorated house. More than likely the warm memories that remain were of the time that is shared, the memories created while catching snowflakes on your tongue, sipping hot chocolate after making snow angels, piling in the living room on blankets and pillows for the annual screening of "The Grinch", or watching the snow fall like diamonds in the purple veil of night.

Allow yourself the space to breathe, to be gentle with yourself and to be where you are. You may or may not be "Merry", and that is okay.

May you be held in the magic of the season.

May the warmth and love of those in your life hold you close as you heal.

May your brokenness feel a little less sharp.

May your tears bring healing and hope and may your heart find the healing that it seeks.

Even when the darkness feels so complete, when the nights feel so long and the light feels so far away.

Know there are moments of joy, of light, of what is to come.

Be open to it all… the darkness and the light and the gray in-between.

Too often we only want to experience the darkness without remembering what Kahlil Gibran reminds us "The deeper that sorrow carves into your being, the more joy you can contain." We like to forgo the darkness and sorrow and skip straight to the light and joy. It feels more comfortable, it often feels preferable, but it is not a wholehearted life.

To hold the darkness at bay requires so much energy. To continually run from what we do not want to feel or experience for fear it will overtake us is exhausting. And when grief and expectations sap us of our energy and the ability to hold the darkness at bay, it can feel like a personal failing.

Instead, understand it is not about will, it is not about "rising above it" it is instead often a learning to live with it, an invitation for grief to join you at the table.

When grief is invited in…
it is then that it loses its power over you,
it is then that grief offers itself to share its gifts.
It is then that there is space made for joy.

When we spend so much time and energy holding the emotions we don't want to feel at bay our hands are not open to receive the emotions we want to feel. We miss the gift of expanding to allow ourselves the fullness of it all. We miss the moments within grief that help to buoy us through, and give us just enough oomph to make it to the next place. It is from this place of respite where we can catch our breath and perhaps begin to see a glimpse of our "new normal".

When we begin to trust the process of grief, of trusting ourselves, of believing that there will come a day when we won't be so consumed by loss and the heaviness, we make space for glimmers of hope. Like the Christmas lights that break through the dark nights of winter we see a little glimmer of light, of hope, of a more balanced life.

A life that doesn't forget our loss-
but also that invites us to once again participate in the land of the living.

One step at a time.

It takes time, often much longer than we would like it to… and especially during the holidays we are reminded of it all. The joy of being together and the ache of knowing that everyone won't be there. The warmth of being together with those we don't see much of the year and the cold reminder that the door will not open with their smiling face on the other side. Simultaneously soaking in the traditions love and laughter and yet a numb, hollow place in your heart where grief seems to have taken root.

Perhaps it is advisable to take the holidays a bit more slowly this year, with more intention, sitting down and truly asking yourself some of these questions:

What do I think I can handle?

How much energy do I have?

How can I take better care of myself in this midst of this season?

- Am I drinking enough water?
- Should I limit my alcohol or sugar intake this year?
- Am I getting enough rest/time for reflection?
- Am I honoring what I need?
- Am I willing to put myself and my grief first when needed?
- Am I surrounding myself with comfort? People, places and things that provide a safe space to be, to breathe, to heal?

Some questions to ask yourself and your family:

What traditions do I want to continue?

What traditions do we want to let go of.. maybe only for this year?

What new traditions do I want to begin?

How would my loved one want us to spend this time?

What is important to me during this season?

Who can support us?

How do I want to honor my grieving heart?

What ways can we weave the spirit and life of our loved one into our time together?

What can I do to help invite and allow joy back into my life?

Joy will often find its way into your heart through little cracks, little moments when you will feel the presence of your loved one, or be reminded of their sense of humor, their laughter, their warm hug. For a moment instead of feeling sad you might feel joy or a lightness of being. Allow yourself to fully embrace those moments as well. Often while traveling the grief journey we feel odd about moments of joy or the first few times you truly laugh again. Sometimes it feels strange, foreign at first. That is okay. It is okay to stick a toe back into the land of the living a bit at a time.

I wrote in my journal about the struggle to find joy again, and the long process to reacquaint myself with that emotion. There is a vulnerability in joy, in letting yourself feel something that you know can be taken so swiftly away. It takes a lot of courage to laugh again, to allow yourself joy and gratitude.

> "A part of you dies with that person, and it is the journey back to life that sometimes hurts the most. The deep, swift cut of death is done; it is learning to live again that is painful.
>
> It is difficult to stop the idea that somehow because they are not here to laugh that we shouldn't either, even if the logical part of you knows that they would want you to laugh, or that they are there laughing with you. To laugh again feels like a betrayal of the highest order. To live the first day where your thoughts weren't constantly on him what he would be doing, thinking, to feel more than the murky numb darkness that has covered the depth and width of your days for so long, to feel that glimmer of hope that maybe you will be okay, maybe you will create a new normal and then the instinctive jumping back into what is now more comfortable, more known, the darkness that feels so complete."

One of the biggest disservices that we do to grief is to not allow it all. We assume we can't lead a full life in the midst of it. You don't have to just do one thing, or one way… you can dance and grieve, you can laugh and grieve… what is right for one person may not be for another. We do ourselves (and others harm) when we judge grief. We judge ourselves and others for grieving too slowly, or too fast, for feeling too much or not enough, for not "doing" it right… whatever that means. Drop the judgement and invite the full experience in.

> *A larger more open possibility is that grief is not mutually exclusive from living your life. You can do anything and grieve. You can laugh with friends and share tears. Grief is one layer of life. It can touch everything we do. It can shift perspectives and priorities. But grief does not happen to the exclusion of all other things.*
>
> *Creative Grief Studio- Cath Duncan*

Grief is hard, it is heavy, it is overwhelming…and it is also surprising.

People are often surprised by the way of quickly breaking your life open in a way that prioritizes things swiftly. Things that we thought were supposed to matter no longer do and people often feel closer to their authentic selves in a way that is unexpected, and often welcome.

People who have been given a terrifying diagnosis, have experienced a car accident or some other significant traumatic event frequently talk about how much clarity it brings. They will say how in an odd way it makes things incredibly simple, and everything is distilled to the core.

Grief strips us bare. It strips us of all of the masks we wear, reminds us how many of us instinctively try to please everyone else at the expense of ourselves. It reminds us of our incredible humanity, our vulnerability and fragility, how much we rely on each other, and how connected we truly are.

Take this new awareness and tenderness that grief can bring and let that spill out into other areas of your life. Treat yourself gently, but also treat the world gently. While walking through grief we see things through new eyes, and often we are able to see pain and suffering in others that we might have overlooked or avoided before. We are opened to the world in new ways and this is both exciting and terrifying.

Yes, we are incredibly fragile and broken and wounded… and yet we love again, we risk losing everyone and everything simply to love, to laugh, to live again…

and we are able to see how strong we really are.

I remember attending a grief group with a therapist who asked those gathered "What strengths can you lean on? When have you felt lost and broken before? How did you survive it?" It seemed so silly to ask about strengths when I felt so small and fragile, so overcome by grief. And yet, that watered a seed in my soul that perhaps I was stronger than I realized. That perhaps I could apply the skills and experiences that had stretched me before to this situation too. Perhaps I was as A. A. Milne reminds us through Pooh Bear "Braver than you believe, stronger than you seem, and smarter than you think."

2 YOUR PERMISSION SLIP

If you are in the midst of grief:

You have permission to not say "Merry Christmas."

You have permission to be frustrated, to be hurt and to be upset by well-meaning friends and family who don't understand the depth of your pain, the place you are in or the difficulty this season might bring.

You have permission for the lights, the decorations, the songs that are meant to bring hope and joy instead to sting your heart and illuminate the gap between what you "want" and what you have.

You have permission to cling to the love of those that surround you, to take more than you give.

You have permission to trust that someday you will be able to give again when life fills you and it is your turn to support, to offer hope, to be the light. You have permission for that time not to be now.

You have permission to feel great love in the midst of great loss.

You have permission to miss that person, place or thing that you have lost - while holding a space in your heart for the possibility of what is yet to come.

And for those who are grieving the loss of someone you love… You have permission to say their name, to bring up in conversation the memories, the love, the loss that you feel.

You have permission to cry and to laugh and to remember and to share those memories.

You have permission to feel anger. Anger at the loss, anger at the changes you see in yourself, in others. Anger that you are now forced to take on new roles, new responsibilities, new challenges that you didn't sign up for.

You have permission to feel numb.

You have permission to simply make it through. To have your celebration be that you did it, somehow, some way, you made it through. Not elegantly, not with any flourish, but instead without fanfare, without makeup or fancy ribbons or bows. Slogging through one day at a time.

You have permission to lose yourself in the elegance, in the beauty, in the meaning of the season. Perhaps you can feel it all. Maybe this year is poignant, and somehow time seems suspended and there is a shimmer to the air that you just can't quite describe. Perhaps this is the year you feel closer than ever to love.

You have permission for this to be a magical Christmas.

Where for the first time you truly feel yourself in Mary's fear, trepidation and bravery.

Maybe you identify with the vulnerability of baby Jesus in a way that catches you completely off guard.

Perhaps this is the year that a young couple traveling by donkey in an unforgiving place, to a place where they are not welcomed, but instead given the lowest of places to try to rest reminds you of your perilous journey over the past year.

Perhaps you find yourself completely overcome by the parallels and the peace that passes all understanding.

Perhaps this year you feel closer than ever to the angels, to the traditions and the memories of past Christmases that wrap you tightly in the goodness of the season. This could be the year you are more grateful than ever for the gifts of tradition and the knowledge that at least something isn't completely different. You may be grateful that you are still the bringer of the best apple pie, or the sweet potato casserole everyone clamors for. Thankful that not everything has shifted in this topsy-turvy year.

You have permission to not know where you are. To feel all or none of these things in rapid succession. Some days may leave you feeling like you are a human ping pong ball. You find yourself moving from one feeling to the next all the while feeling a bit off kilter. **You have permission not to be "Merry".**

3 SUPPORTING OTHERS IN THE MIDST OF GRIEF:

There are so many ways to help someone who is hurting. But there are a few things I have heard time and time again from every person, in every grief group. Two simple things that everyone longs for from others who are walking alongside- acknowledgement and naming.

Acknowledge the struggle that this season may bring.

You don't have to say anything fancy, you don't even have to know what to say… it is enough to say "this must be hard", or "I'm here if you need to talk, I'm sure this is a roller coaster of a time for you." "I know this Christmas, this first must be hard for you. Have you thought about what might bring the most healing for you?" or "I can remember the first Christmas after my grandma passed away, it was really hard. We made it special by everyone mentioning a favorite memory of them. Would you like to do something like that this year?"

Say their name. Say the name of those we have lost knowing that your acknowledgment may bring tears, but know that is a part of the healing Your remembering soothes our heart. Hearing their name keeps the memory, the spirit of the person alive, it keeps them present, especially in a moment when we are desperate to have them with us.

Ask us to share memories of those that we have lost, allow us the opportunities to remember the love, the laughter and the memories. Allow us space to keep the love alive in our heart.

Allow us to keep things the same or the freedom to do things entirely differently this year. Ask us what we need- and then listen. Give us space when we say "we don't know" or honor our request when we find the courage to say "I would like to do things differently this year".

Know that it may be a roller coaster… laughter may turn to tears, and tears may turn to laughter. It can feel scary to feel so out of control when grief takes the reins. You can bring us great comfort when you remind us that we are loved through it all.

Don't try to take the pain away… it can feel like you aren't honoring our loss, or that you don't care, even when you do. Sometimes feeling the pain is the closest we can come to holding tight to our loved ones and when people try to take that away too it is too much.

Know that your presence is a gift in and of itself.

Know that we may cling to you for the love and light we are looking for – and yet you are not solely responsible for making us "Merry".

Know that even though it doesn't take the place of what was lost **your love is enough.**

Your desire to help matters, your belief that we will get through this time and that we don't have to walk through it alone means the world.

"If you want to help a person in grief, accept you can't just remove their heartache. By even trying to erase someone's pain, you are telling them you believe it to be fixable. Loss is never fixable. Grief is neve erasable. So simply walk with them as their hearts begin to heal, and show them patience, kindness and loving acceptance."

Zoe Clark-Coates

ROCKINGHAM
SCHOOL

4 A PASS AND A PRAYER FOR THE FIRST CHRISTMAS

Dear one,

This complicates things so much. It wasn't the plan, it wasn't the way it was supposed to be,

and yet… here we are.

You may wonder how you will get through the day, how you are ever to smile again, much less be "Merry".

Just don't.

For one Christmas just don't. If you don't want to put up a tree, don't.

If you don't want to send out Christmas cards, don't.

If you can't bring yourself to read other people's Christmas cards, don't.

And by all means if you want to do it all exactly the same as you always have done, do it!

But, perhaps, for this Christmas, you will give yourself a pass.

Let your expectations drop,

focus on the love that remains,

focus on the memories, and pay attention to the pain.

Don't hide it, don't shove it underneath a strained "Merry Christmas", don't drown it in too much liquor or lull it into a sugar coma with too many sweets.

Your pain is inviting you to pay attention.

Your heart has been through so much, it has been torn, bruised and battered this year.

It is time to rest, to repair, to heal. But in order to do that you must be willing to pay attention to the pain- which we so often avoid.

I remember sitting on the bed crying, wondering if it was possible for my heart to literally break because I was so sure I was feeling more pain than my heart could hold.

Now I know. Yes, the grief manifests itself physically in so many ways. It robs us of our energy, our desire to engage in our lives in the same way and oftentimes interferes with our ability to see the joy in things. What was once a colorful life becomes like living in a black and white world.

At the time, I wondered if I was going crazy. And yet I heard this time and time again.

Dear one,

You are not going crazy,

you have loved much and this loss runs deep.

I didn't know what I know now…

that our hearts are amazing,

they are far more powerful than we even realize,

and sometimes when it feels like it is breaking –

it is breaking-

breaking open

to allow more room for more love, more joy, more gratitude,

and the process can be quite painful.

You are allowed to grieve, to have your time, to have this Christmas be a jumbled mess of everything. Joy, sadness, gratitude, love and perhaps even a moment (or more) where it the grief doesn't feel quite so heavy anymore.

To the extent that you can **"don't anticipate, participate".**

Anticipating when grief will hit is like trying to catch a wave in your hand, it just doesn't work.

You will sail by moments you thought you weren't going to make it through and then something else will hit you that you never expected. Sometimes the worst part is leading up to the event or milestone and anticipating what it might be like and on that day there is simply a dull numbness. Sometimes it sneaks up from behind or surprises us when we least expect it.

Grief isn't linear and can't be treated as such, it is a wild mess of jumbled things that can't be anticipated. However, if you participate, if you buckle yourself in for this wild ride, if you allow yourself to fully feel it you will gain trust in yourself again that yes, you can ride this wave, you can do this.

You may not know how, but you can.

You only need to get through this moment. Chemically speaking, emotions only last 90 seconds. The waves appear, rise up, crest and recede. If you can make it through 90 seconds you can get through anything. There will be a pause, and you can catch your breath until the next wave. And pretty soon the waves aren't quite so constant.

One moment at a time.

That first Christmas my mantra was from the Amy Grant song "Breath of Heaven"

Breath of heaven
Hold me together
Be forever near me…

I invite you to pick a phrase, a lyric, a verse, something that will get you through, something for those moments that you need to focus on getting through to the next wave.

Here are a few things I know to be true…

You will be held. In the midst of your darkest night, there will be someone, something that will remind you that you are not alone.

You will make it through this day. It may not be pretty, it may not be what you anticipated, but it will be over. Hour by hour, minute by minute, you will get through this.

You have the right to turn down invitations, to decide what is healthiest for you, ***without buying into other's expectations or guilt.***

It is imperative that you listen to your own grief journey, to listen to what your heart needs.

Know there are others who understand, who have been where you are. They may travel the journey differently, or faster or more slowly than you. This is not a contest, it is not a race.

Your grief journey is unique to you. Part of the journey is to rebuild trust in your process, in your intuition, in your ability to find your way through the darkness.

Know that my heart is outstretched to yours and I am holding a candle to light the darkness.

My prayer for you:

May you be held, may you be loved, may you find peace wherever you are.

ERICA STAAB

5 GENTLE REMINDERS

There is a sacredness in tears. They are not the mark of weakness, but of power. They speak more eloquently than ten thousand tongues. They are messengers of overwhelming grief, of deep contrition, and of unspeakable love.

Washington Irving

Let your tears flow. Too often we try to stifle them, or not share them. We are better in all ways when we allow ourselves to cry. There are physical, emotional and psychological ramifications if we don't allow ourselves to cry and release all of the energy emotion that we are holding deep within. It may be scary because it feels like the tears will never stop. I promise, they will.

Ask others who have lost loved ones, time doesn't heal all things, but it does change them.

Some of the ways that people have gotten through:

One of my friends invited each person in their family to bring an ornament that reminds them of her husband She puts up a little tree with all of the special ornaments up each year. For the first year she left it up though the year since it brought her great joy and peace. To both be reminded of him and reminded of all of the love and support that surrounded her.

Another friend sets the table to include the person they have lost and each year they save a seat for them.

Some dress up in flannel, cameo or their loved ones favorite team jersey when they gather together for the family Christmas.

Hire out the cooking. This year perhaps you take a drive to the local restaurant that stays open Christmas Eve and you leave the cooking and the clean up to someone else. Or have a pizza party and break out the frozen pizza. Give yourself a pass this year.

Unless…

Unless making your favorite Jell-O dish is exactly what you need. And maybe sharing your love through your famous chocolate crinkle cookies that everyone requests each year is a way of giving back some of the love you have been soaking in from your family.

This might be the year you make your Aunt's favorite cookies and copy the recipe with her handwriting to share with everyone.

Give money in your loved ones name to their favorite charities in lieu of presents, leave the shopping to someone else, or do all of your shopping online.

Unless…

Unless picking out the perfect gift, sewing a quilt using your dad's ties, making a teddy bear from your daughter's favorite sweatshirt, or creating a photo album for all of the grandkids to remember grandma by is what brings you joy and healing.

Build in time for naps. Grief is a physical thing. Your body will need more time to rest and recover.

Think about what fills you and what drains you. Do more of what fills and heals your heart.

Take it one event at a time. Give yourself permission to skip things if it doesn't seem like it would be a good fit, and yet at the same time give yourself permission to go to something with the intention of leaving early… you might just find it is exactly what you need.

> *Grief, I've learned, is really just love. It is all the love you want to give, but cannot. All that unspent love gathers up in the corners of your eyes, the lump in your throat, and in the hollow part of your chest.*

Grief is just love with no place to go.

Jamie Anderson

Stay open to the magic of the season.

Woven in between the tears, the questions and the heartache will be moments of peace, snippets of joy and love that will carry you through. Ask for help from others who have walked this journey before you. Take what fits for you and leave the rest. Your journey is yours alone. You will have friends walk alongside you for parts of it. There will be acquaintances and strangers who will show up and be angels at just the right time in ways you could not even imagine. Ultimately your path is unique to you, your loved one and the love you shared, but you are never alone. To be human is to love, to lose and to find some way to carry on.

You will make it through. One moment at a time.